The N.O.W. Experience:
720* DEGREE TURN

Dr. Edward Hamilton

The N.O.W. Experience: 720* DEGREE TURN

Dedication

This book is dedicated to the one that is stuck in yesterday, the one that has given up on themselves, the one that thought it was over, and the one that sees no future.

This reading will change your personal life.

Expect to never, ever be the same again and to walk in the excellence that GOD has designed just for you.

The N.O.W. Experience: 720* DEGREE TURN

Foreword

I will start by warning you, dear reader, of the power you now hold in your hands! The author of this book carries an anointing that breaks chains that have kept people bound.

Life's challenges and personal development on his own road to healing has allowed him to first look at himself, admit his issues and take two critical turns in his life that he details in his narration.

Now, after many years of counseling, outreach, ministry, televangelism and Christian broadcast, you will benefit by receiving the raw and uncut version of true methods to a radical transformation.

Dr. Edward Hamilton

The N.O.W. Experience: 720* DEGREE TURN

Dr. Edward Hamilton's book "The N.O.W. Experience" not only educates you, but it also challenges best part of you, your mind. This is a defining moment where your thinking will be stretched to a new level with promising options in the Lord Jesus Christ.

Many people in the world have issues, but the truth is that many do not know that they also have the solutions that were bought and paid for by God. God, the creator, Elohim, left over 7,000 promises to man to have access to abundant life and to experience that life right NOW on earth as it is in heaven. Last, but not least, many of the physical and mental health issues from people on every continent usually start with some form of stress in the mind. Dr. Hamilton teaches you in this

The N.O.W. Experience: 720* DEGREE TURN

book how to strengthen your thought life, recognize a pattern or cycle of disfunction and he then leads you to several different practical steps to overcome the battle that appeared impossible. Many of them are just fears. Yes, false evidence appearing real (F.E.A.R.). Dr. Edward Hamilton reminds the reader to receive the wholeness that Jesus Christ has paid a price for and to start the new life that has never been seen or experienced before.

Congratulations, you are a seeker of wholeness and wholeness is what you will find here and right NOW.

Enjoy!

P2P Covenant Partners of the world

The N.O.W. Experience: 720* DEGREE TURN

Acknowledgments

First, I want to acknowledge my Lord and Savior, Jesus Christ, whom I am nothing without, but with Him, I am everything He has called me to be. Thank you, Father God, for your constant love and patience with me.

Thank you to my P2P The N.O.W. Church & Network, SWAG, Vertical Leap families for your constant motivation to never quit or give up and your support in finishing this project.

To my children and grandchildren, who have taught me love and patience through life's issues and true forgiveness through God truly loving one another.

The N.O.W. Experience: 720* DEGREE TURN

To my mentors, Coach Al & Coach Hatti Hollingsworth - Thank you for being the support system that loved me till I made it. Thank you both for your vision that has touched the world with hope and purpose. Please continue to teach and motivate as we are paying attention!

To Bishop Herald & Dr. Mary Jackson - Your advice and encouragement have been most appreciated and without you in my life...ohhh, well you already know 😊.

To the reader – I am so glad to finally present this book to you. Thank you for taking a chance on this project and supporting my ministry in reaching the lost and unsaved as well as those who desire to go higher in life and have a renewed mind.

Dr. Edward Hamilton

The N.O.W. Experience: 720* DEGREE TURN

Table of Contents

The N.O.W. Credo

The Beginning of the Experience

Chapter 1: Changing the Way We Think

Chapter 2: Changing Directions NOW

Chapter 3: It is War!

Chapter 4: Faith

Chapter 5: The Turn

Chapter 6: Beliefs-Thoughts-Feelings

The N.O.W. Experience: 720* DEGREE TURN

The N.O.W. CREDO

1. Today is my day for change!

I will not be conformed to this world, for I am NOW (0 – 5 seconds) transformed by the renewing of my mind.

2. I will live in my N.O.W. 0 – 5 seconds daily. Taking up my cross and following the steps that have been ordered by the Lord; activating His favor, seeking, asking and knocking on all doors to be opened unto me.

The N.O.W. Experience: 720* DEGREE TURN

3. No longer will I live my life as a victim. I will stand firm and resist the wiles of the enemy because I am more than a conqueror through Christ who strengthens me.

4. Equipped in my new life in Christ, I will prepare for the battle daily as I follow Christ putting on my whole armor of God that I may be able to stand in His righteousness and glory.

5. With my birthrights intact: confidence, courage, hope, belief, faith, and trust, I commit to my purpose in God, to go, to search, to teach and to make disciples.

The N.O.W. Experience: 720* DEGREE TURN

6. In line with my purpose and connected to my Source; I will abide in the Lord at all times, standing on His promise; for He will abide in me if I seek first His kingdom and righteousness above any other.

7. Commitment, dedication, and strength come only from God. I will walk in His counsel daily and follow His statues with all my heart so that I may be found pleasing in His sight.

8. Because Christ lives in me and I in Him, no longer will I live according to my past, but looking forward to the

The N.O.W. Experience: 720* DEGREE TURN

mark of my high calling, I will live victoriously in Christ.

9. With my mind set on these things, my life will be an example of truth, honesty, purity, love and good report of Jesus.

10. With love in my heart and God as my Source, I will walk with a spirit of expectancy, believing in God's word and trusting His promises to perform with confidence that it's already done.

The N.O.W. Experience: 720* DEGREE TURN

The Beginning of the Experience

Now has been defined as 0-5 seconds where we can obtain a GOD given dream, vision or idea before it passes into memory. The bible teaches us (Hebrews 11:1) that NOW faith is the substance of things hoped for and the evidence of things not seen. This is where we as followers of Christ must develop the lifestyle of walking by faith and not by sight (2 Corinthians 5:7) and become provoked by the Holy Spirit!

The N.O.W. Experience: 720* DEGREE TURN

Family, to be provoked to purpose is simply being called forth to do or to act. 2 Corinthians 9:2 states "and your zeal hath provoked very many." Paul is saying to the Corinthians that their zeal has stirred up similar zeal on the part of the people of Macedonia. Hebrews 10:24 tells us "And let us consider one another to provoke unto love and to good works."

These scriptures are instructing us to think of ways to motivate, stir up, or provoke one another to love and do

The N.O.W. Experience: 720* DEGREE TURN

good works. We should be motivated, stirred up, provoked, and incited to find our desired goal and purpose. However, many of us have put our purpose on the back burner due to family, relationships, school or careers. We search a lifetime wondering if we are living or doing what we have been called to do. Listen, time waits for no one and neither will God. Yet, we continue to waste precious time, pondering, making excuses and choosing not to go the extra mile to avoid the pain and suffering that comes from going through the necessary trails

The N.O.W. Experience: 720* DEGREE TURN

of life. We find ourselves settling for what's available. Never seeking and searching for that God-given purpose for our God purposed life.

We find ourselves off the path from a purpose driven life. We willingly endure problems that produce worldly gifts that lead us or guide us away from the guidance of God, which causes us to fail mightily. Our circumstances can be changed with God's help if we begin to expect His presence and His blessings in our lives. But guess what we do? We

The N.O.W. Experience: 720* DEGREE TURN

still wait for God's blessings. We say we believe in His son Jesus. We say that we have special gifts. We say that we have an inheritance through Him to receive spiritual blessings. We also say that sin can no longer dominate our thoughts or our choices because of Christ.

However, we do not reach out to receive these blessings, that is when we are defeated, and our Godly purpose is lost. Friends, we must actively seek to know what our purpose is and to live the God predestined life that is ordered by Him.

So, the question may be how? How do we become transformed to God's perfect will? The first thing I'll share is that we must begin all over and allow God to have His way in and through our lives. That means we must be provoked to our purpose in Christ Jesus, acknowledging that it's only by and through Him that we can accomplish this goal. With Him, nothing is impossible. The next question might be who can be provoked?

The Bible states in 2 Corinthians 5:17 "Therefore, if any man be in Christ, he is a new creature: old things are passed away; behold all things are become new." The answer is easy! Anyone can be provoked if we are in Him who strengthens us. It is very important that we begin to believe God's word and process it as truth and become new creations, new creatures, the new man, or the new woman that the word says

The N.O.W. Experience: 720* DEGREE TURN

we can be. Let all those old things pass away so that they can become new. We must believe all things are of God and that through Him, we have the inheritance to claim these blessings. Also, we must believe that we are ambassadors of Christ and that God will work through us if we submit to Him. It was God that made Jesus who knew no sin to come and die for ours that we could become the righteousness of God.

From this point forward, we are going to walk through some vital principles that

The N.O.W. Experience: 720* DEGREE TURN

you can implement NOW to begin to experience your God purposed life.

As we begin our journey of The NOW experience, the first step is to ensure you bond with GOD as our personal Lord and Savior. If you're reading this and you don't know JESUS, Stop and Call the P2P Community Development (562) 413-3710 and receive JESUS, right NOW!

Chapter 1
Changing the Way We Think!

Family the brain is where we must begin changing the way we think. We begin our journey with the brain to understand where the battle starts. The thinking process must be focused because the enemy is attempting to rob, kill and destroy our bond with the one Jesus (John 10:10). It is important to stay open to God's word and keep our minds fixed on Jesus so we can withstand the wickedness of the enemy.

The N.O.W. Experience: 720* DEGREE TURN

What is in our minds determines what comes out in our actions, our mouth, and emotions. We must stay willing to listen and understand God's ways that He so clearly explains. God will put His laws in our minds, which will produce understanding.

Proverbs 23:7 – "as a man thinketh in his heart
(mind) so is he." We must keep our mind working the principle in order to change the way we think.

The N.O.W. Experience: 720* DEGREE TURN

The brain is a muscle that requires exercise and must stay connected to the source of everything. The source of everything is God. The brain is a large mass of cells and nerve tissue that is responsible for the interpretation of sensor impulses, the thought process, and our body's emotions. We can call this our hard drive. God desires our focus and attention in our thinking process, and therefore our thinking process must change drastically. The Word shows us example after example of how His mind must be in us.

The N.O.W. Experience: 720* DEGREE TURN

There are three different ways to use our brain to give our attention/listening to a matter or subject.

1. Selective Attention: We hear only what is good for our ears and we tune in to only what applies to me, me, and me.

2. Pretend Attention: We are there in body only. Our focus is elsewhere, daydreaming and not hearing a single word. Lost with no direction.

The N.O.W. Experience: 720* DEGREE TURN

3. Focused Attention: this is exactly where God wants us to be. Giving our full attention so that we can receive knowledge, wisdom and understanding from Him. This will build our beliefs, our thoughts, and our feelings. This is where we win if we stay focused.

The brain is divided into two parts, the conscious mind, and the subconscious mind.

The N.O.W. Experience: 720* DEGREE TURN

The conscious mind combines the mind, soul, and spirit. This is where we can be able to define truth and reality. The subconscious mind combines the mind and body. This is where we are led to make our decisions from things of this world, and this is where the battle begins.

The conscious mind and the subconscious mind are at war. This battle between both sides of our brain is in total control of information acquired, saved and used to make decisions in our

The N.O.W. Experience: 720* DEGREE TURN

lives for today. The bible says in James 1:8 that, "a double minded man is unstable in all his ways", and again also in Proverbs 23:7 the word says, "that as a man thinketh in his heart (mind) so is he." This is clearly telling us that whatever we put in our brains is most likely what will come out.

There are some simple facts that we will learn about our brain that may amaze the best of us:

The N.O.W. Experience: 720* DEGREE TURN

- The brain is temporal, and its function is automatically set to sustain our survival
- The brain can be considered the hard drive of our thinking
- The brain could be considered the center of the body
- The brain is where all personal truth and reality are defined and confirmed
- The brain is where we have the ability to discern good from evil and truth from false

The N.O.W. Experience: 720* DEGREE TURN

- The brain has the capacity to process over 100 million bytes of information per second
- The brain has the capacity to store all the information written and recorded and would still have 75% storage capacity remain
- The brain has the potential to increase these capacities with proper exercise

These are great facts, but the truth of the matter is that God has called us to be spiritual beings not physical. That's

The N.O.W. Experience: 720* DEGREE TURN

why the word of God says in, Romans 12:2 that we should, "be not conformed to this world, but be ye transformed by the renewing of your mind." God is instructing us to begin to think Godly, to live Godly, and to act Godly. We must realize that this war we spoke of earlier is an ongoing battle in our minds where we are required of God to fight the good fight of faith to be rooted in and grounded in Him all the time – 1 Timothy 6:11. Our focus must be on Him 24/7, 365 days of the year waging war to win the battle. We are further

The N.O.W. Experience: 720* DEGREE TURN

instructed not to be conformed to this world, meaning that when we are led by our subconscious mind, we will be led by worldly standards and not His. There are five categories of our subconscious that will lead us to lose the battle and die of this world:

1. Being led by our 5 senses
    a. Smell, sight, touch, taste, and hearing
2. Being led by our intuition

The N.O.W. Experience: 720* DEGREE TURN

    a. Defining truth without conscious attention or reasoning

3. Being led by our culture or tradition

    a. Continuing to do things as we always have.

4. Being led by authority figures

    a. Government, religious leaders, or experts.

5. Being led by our reasoning

    a. The influence of our rational thinking.

Through these categories we make our decisions. The enemy leads us to destruction when we rely on these categories to make decisions.

Additionally, being led by these categories cannot be trusted and will lead to death. The word of God in John 10:10 says that, "the thief comes but to kill steal and destroy..." To kill God's plan and purpose for our lives, to steal our focus from God and His word and destroy our commitment to God and what He has called us to do.

The enemy would love nothing better than to block God's communication to

The N.O.W. Experience: 720* DEGREE TURN

His people, so we do not hear, see, do and live the word correctly. The enemy is not here to recruit us to his service; his main goal is to distract our attention from God's purpose for us. The enemy likes to be in the battleground of our minds to keep us operating in our past failures where we will never grow any further than our past. We must let go of past failures, past toxic relationships, past failed business ventures or past losses. If we live in our past failures, we will die and never find our true purpose in the Lord.

The N.O.W. Experience: 720* DEGREE TURN

We can win and begin to live again if we choose life in Christ and allow God to lead and guide us not into temptation but delivering us from evil (Matthew 6:13). We must become seekers of God's truth. We must constantly seek first the kingdom of God and all His righteousness. Our goal is to be all that we can be in Him so we can win this fight of faith. We must make right choices, the right decisions, choosing the right ways of doing things through Christ who strengthens us, and we shall be overtaken by blessings everywhere and abundantly. The word of God says in Matthew 6:33 that we are to, "**seek** ye first the kingdom of God and His righteousness and all things shall be added unto you." This means that no longer can we expect the easy road, but we must

begin to walk in His principles and become **more than** conquerors through Jesus (Romans 8:37).

Now we can truly begin again, live again and serve God on earth as it is in heaven and get in line with God's finished work. In the Lord's Prayer it says that kingdom come, will be done on earth as it **is** in heaven. Notice that the word states that it's already done, and God will manifest the ordering of our steps. We must line up with His work on earth as He has already finished or completed the work in heaven. God sets everything in motion, it is His plan not ours that should be followed and not that of the princes of this world. God has made a covenant with His people that He will

The N.O.W. Experience: 720* DEGREE TURN

put His laws in their minds and write them on their hearts, and I will be their God and they shall be my people (Hebrews 8:10). God has promised to do something spectacular for His people. He shall download lots of information into our hard drives (the brain) of our bodies (remember shall is a promise). God has given us direct divine instructions on how to find our Godly purpose and to live here on earth. To top that off He sent His only begotten son Jesus so we can find our purpose and have life and

The N.O.W. Experience: 720* DEGREE TURN

life more abundantly (John 10:10). The word of God says in Jeremiah 31:34 that, "no longer shall every man teach his neighbor and his brother saying know the Lord, for they shall know me from the least to the greatest of them says the Lord for I will forgive their iniquity, and their sin I will remember no more." We must live on His word and fight the battle at hand which is to choose to walk after the spirit not the flesh, which is weak (Matthew 26:41). We must think clearly so that our mediating will be acceptable to Him. We

The N.O.W. Experience: 720* DEGREE TURN

must be renewed by the spirit of the mind, having a sound mind renewed by knowledge. We must have the full confidence that it **shall** be done as you have believed.

The Zone is where we stay connected to God. This is where God's favor and anointing separates us from this world and connects us to Him and His covering of grace. This is where we can do all things through Jesus Christ who strengthens us freely to battle the wiles of the enemy. Now the battle really begins and ends where we have the

The N.O.W. Experience: 720* DEGREE TURN

power to fight, stand and win. God's word clearly states in 2 Timothy 1:7, that we "...have not been given a spirit of fear, but of power and love and of sound mind", becoming Godly thinkers through Christ. For one, who has known the mind of the Lord that he may instruct Him? So, we have the mind of Christ to do the work we have been purposed with, to live as He did, holy and blameless, constantly in prayer for guidance from our Father so that we make right choices (1 Corinthians 2:16). We are the body of Christ that has the

The N.O.W. Experience: 720* DEGREE TURN

perfect opportunity to change the way we think that will then lead to our choices being like Christ.

In Philippians 2:5 it says that we should, "let this mind be in you, which was also in Christ Jesus." This is when we do not think the way we use to think, but we begin to change and let His word start to take over our minds. We should begin to know Him and the power of His resurrection and the fellowship of His suffering. Being conformed to His death and truly begin to live and find our God given purpose in life (Philippians 3:10).

The N.O.W. Experience: 720* DEGREE TURN

If we live and walk daily with the Lord through His example, we will experience firsthand how to think as He did. The word says, greater is He that lives in me than the evil in this world. The world will attempt to conform and influence us to do things the world's way. Remember, we have been called to stay focused on Him and not doubt God's word.

As we become conscious in our thinking, our soul and spirit shall lead us through our conscious thinking through these steps:

The N.O.W. Experience: 720* DEGREE TURN

- Recognition – pay close attention to and be aware
- Identification – establish, associate or group things in their right categories
- Organization – to arrange by planning things in an exact category
- Filing – to put away for future reference and destroy unwanted memories and experiences

As we become thinkers like Christ and take in information, we can use these methods to gather and to organize what

The N.O.W. Experience: 720* DEGREE TURN

is good and not good and then choose what's to be used for now or future use. We begin to realize that all information is not useful and needs to be erased from our thinking.

In Philippians 3:12-14 the word says that, not as though I had already attained, either was already perfect: but I follow, if that I may apprehend that for which also I am apprehended of Christ Jesus. [13]Brethren, I count not myself to have apprehended: but *this* one thing *I do*, forgetting those things which are behind, and reaching forth unto those

The N.O.W. Experience: 720* DEGREE TURN

things which are before, [14]I press toward the mark for the prize of the high calling of God in Christ Jesus.

Some would ask, Now is the place in time (0 – 5 seconds) where the conscious mind can retain a God-given dream, thought or idea from heaven before passing it into past memory. That is why it imperative to stay connected to our source of Godly protection. One mind with Christ, steadfast showing ourselves approved staying in the game because of His knowledge. Walking bold, not giving to the spirit of fear, but of power, love, and a sound mind. This is the area where God operates in our consciousness for the giving of instruction for a Godly purposed driven life. The word also tells us in Hebrews 11:1 that "Now faith is the substance of things hoped for and the evidence of things not seen". Not yesterday faith. Not tomorrow faith. The word says, "**<u>Now</u>** faith." This is where we can move when God says move, then we can speak when God says speak. Then and

The N.O.W. Experience: 720* DEGREE TURN

only then are we what God has called us to be through Christ Jesus, where we can be provoked unto purpose right Now. Most of us have this ten-year plan to have our own way of getting to God, have fun now seek God later, but God has called us to move and find our purpose right now before the opportunity is over. Begin today by exercising the first principle of changing the way you think.

The N.O.W. Experience: 720* DEGREE TURN

Chapter 2
Changing Directions NOW.!

Family we have seen from step one, how to change the way we think and to think as Christ would. His mind is in us and with new purpose and desire we should begin to follow His example. In the word, 1 Peter 2:21 tells us that, "for to this you were called, because Christ also suffered for us, leaving us an example, that you should follow His steps". Recognize here that it is no longer our way, our desires but His

The N.O.W. Experience: 720* DEGREE TURN

purpose, way and will that we should be consumed with.

In John 3:30, the word tells us that He must increase, but we must decrease. Meaning that we must let the lesser things die so the greater may live. Then we can come into balance with Him, being aware that our spirit is that of Christ and our flesh is of the world. On the road to His purpose, Jesus was bothered with His flesh about having to die for the sins of this world. As time came closer to the decision of death,

The N.O.W. Experience: 720* DEGREE TURN

Jesus fell on His knees to pray. In Matthew 26:39, the word tells of how He went a little farther and fell on His face, and prayed, saying, "O My Father, if it is possible, let this cup pass from Me; nevertheless, not as I will, but as You *will.*" The Lord gives us a great example of how our human characteristics will dread the pain of having to go through something important to God or concerning following Him. Jesus returned to find His disciples sleeping, but the key is not their weakness, but the fact His flesh was weak, so He returned for intercessors but knelt and prayed to God for guidance. So, we must prepare ourselves for some

resistance, but we can do it if we stay strong in the Lord and the power of His might (Ephesians 6:10). Be willing to go through the circumstances of our newfound purpose in Christ and remember that the enemy does not stop, he will continue to come and block God's word from reaching us. So that is why it is so important to stay connected

The N.O.W. Experience: 720* DEGREE TURN

to God and His word and to take up our cross daily. Follow Him and choose purpose and not death.

But we must avoid the easy route, making excuses around problems and conflicts that cause great pain and where most give up. Look at this example, have you ever been riding your bike and the chain suddenly broke or came off? And as you continued to peddle, you began to slow down and eventually went nowhere? You kept on peddling, still went nowhere and then eventually had to stop before you fell.

Well family that is what will happen to us when we go around life's obstacles or our purpose in life. But if we stay on course in the protection of the Lord, we can withstand the wiles of the enemy and endure the tests, trials, obstacles or rough winds and continue to stay on the course of righteousness following Him who came to save us. The word also tells us in Luke 9:23, Then He said to *them* all, "If anyone desires to come

The N.O.W. Experience: 720* DEGREE TURN

after Me, let him deny himself, and take up his cross daily, and follow Me.

Well get ready because we have some real work to do. Let us look at Apostle Paul as an example of this principle. On the road to Damascus, Paul's purpose was revealed. His own will was broken, torn down and rebuilt in the way God purposed for his life. Through his transformation, he first had to change the way he thought, walked, and talked. He then had to except that he was changed, that his flesh will

The N.O.W. Experience: 720* DEGREE TURN

come against him, and that he would have to experience going *through* circumstances and not around them. Matthew 26:39 teaches that our sinful nature will cause us to doubt and fear, but in (1 Corinthians 3:13-15) it tells us we must find our worth through a time of testing. But Paul learned that what we do before and through our circumstances made the difference compared to what occurred. Staying faithful to God must be more important to us than the pain and suffering that life brings. Look at Christ, His whole

The N.O.W. Experience: 720* DEGREE TURN

being was surrounded by trials, tribulations and going through, but even when fear and doubt set in His flesh He prayed for strength and directions from His source of everything God. His example was to teach us the principle of NOW 0-5 seconds prayer. Pray and pray daily do not quit pray even when you get up to do something so that He can meet us in agreement and see His Glory fulfilled. The word of God says daily. That means no matter what our choices are we must take them up and bear them NOW. Take it up and follow

The N.O.W. Experience: 720* DEGREE TURN

Christ even through the rough times we must lose our lives for Him whom gave His life for us on the cross at Calvary to bear our sins. Understand that now is when our stability of thinking comes into control of our decision making, where we become more than conquerors and overcomers in Christ. But if we are willing to follow Him the word says in Matthew 10:38 "He who finds his life will lose it and he who loses his life for My sake will find it." Jesus has called us to die of ourselves and begin to live for Him. Understanding that we have been predestined to be God's children, and we must praise Him through it all, putting all hope in Him as truth. Let us realize that there is a lot of work ahead of us on this journey of going through for Him. But as we submit to Him, our main goal should be to hear Him, seek Him first and obey His righteousness, then all things will be added unto us. What things? What treasures? What prize? Well, here are a few of those promises:

The N.O.W. Experience: 720* DEGREE TURN

1. How to endure   Matthew 10:22
2. How to overcome   Romans 12:21
3. How to develop patience James 1:4
4. How to have testimony John 21:24

By enduring we will be able sustain the wiles of the enemy and tolerate persecution without falling or stumbling. Then, our experience will teach us how to defeat the enemy. Then, developing patience, we can stand and wait on God's timing and not ours, having faith in God believing all things will work together for our good according to His

The N.O.W. Experience: 720* DEGREE TURN

riches and glory. Jesus took up His cross to give us access to a divine relationship with God, lacking nothing. We must take back what was stolen from the beginning of time – Our Birthrights:

Confidence – 1 John 5:14 ~ In God we are confident that if we ask anything according to His will (purpose), He will hear us.

Courage – Psalms 27:14 ~ Wait on the Lord and be of good courage and He shall strengthen your heart (mind), wait I say on the Lord.

The N.O.W. Experience: 720* DEGREE TURN

Hope – Romans 15:13 ~ Now may the God of hope fill you with all joy and peace in believing, that you may abound in hope by the power of the Holy Spirit.

Belief – Acts 4:32 ~ Now the multiples of those who believed were of one heart and of one soul.

Faith – Hebrews 11:1 ~ Now faith is the substance of things hoped for and the evidence of things not seen.

Trust – Proverbs 3:5 ~ Trust in the Lord with all your heart and lean not upon your own understanding.

The N.O.W. Experience: 720* DEGREE TURN

God has given man the advantage over everything of this world, but because of the mistake of not obeying Him, we lost our advantage and became lost in sin. But because of the sacrifice of Jesus, we can have the advantage back and be fully equipped to fight the good fight of faith. The enemy does not want our confidence to be in the Lord, for us to be courageous, to go to battle hopeful for victory, or believing in Jesus as savior. He does not want us faithful that all things will work together for our good and trusting God that He is the

The N.O.W. Experience: 720* DEGREE TURN

source of everything needed in heaven or on earth. We can and will succeed at our new life in Christ because as we change the way we think we become victorious in Him.

Chapter 3

It is War!

Family NOW that we have found out that our mind is the place where God dwells, where He downloads information and writes them on our hearts, we can now step to the next level. But first, we need to be aware of the exact place where the battle takes place and where spiritual warfare exists. This is where we can finally win this battle with consciousness and live our Godly purposed life victoriously. The word of GOD says in

The N.O.W. Experience: 720* DEGREE TURN

Ephesians 3:16-20, "that He would grant you, according to the riches of His glory, to be strengthened with might through His Spirit in the inner man, [17]that Christ may dwell in your hearts through faith; that you, being rooted and grounded in love, [18]may be able to comprehend with all the saints what *is* the width and length and depth and height - [19]to know the love of Christ which passes knowledge; that you may be filled with all the fullness of God. [20]Now to Him who is able to do exceedingly abundantly above all that we ask or think, according to the power that

The N.O.W. Experience: 720* DEGREE TURN

works in us." This information is self-explanatory, that we must use the knowledge and understanding gained from God through relationship to discern the physical makeup of this world. We must understand that we live in a dimensional universe made up of 5 quadrants. The third dimension, which we dwell in, is made up of all material; things of length, width, depth, and height. How deep, how long and how high as we read in Ephesians earlier. We are instructed to be able to comprehend these principles to stand and win. Now we must understand that God dwells inside of us and is referred to as the inner man. God has shown us that He abides in us that we can bear much fruit. John 15:7 tells us that "If you abide in Me, and My words abide in you, you will ask what you desire, and it shall be done for you." See, we can think and live His way according to His purpose for our lives because He lives in us.

We must also understand that the battle is not ours but the Lord's and has nothing to do with physical fights, but instead

The N.O.W. Experience: 720* DEGREE TURN

with spiritual warfare. We should fight more in our minds than with our fists and prayer is the basis of this battle, inside out, not outside in. As we learned earlier, God is in us so we cannot be conformed to this world. We must abide in the protective zone of God under the anointing and fight. The word says that not by power and might but by the spirit of the Lord. In Ephesians 6:12 it reads, "for we do not wrestle against flesh and blood, but against principalities, against powers, against the rulers of the darkness of this age, against spiritual *hosts* of wickedness in the heavenly *places*."

The fourth dimension is where spirits, principalities and enemies' dwell and to win this battle, this is where we fight! The battle isn't against flesh, but against spirits that live inside flesh. We must understand the war ends and begins on our knees through prayer, praise, and worship in our minds. If we just look close at the example of Jesus, we see that He battled on His knees through every trail. We must begin to follow His

The N.O.W. Experience: 720* DEGREE TURN

example, become prayer warriors because He lives in us and we can do all things through Him that strengthens us. When we learn to concentrate on the things of God, we develop a focal point on Him and only Him. We can only survive by keeping our eyes fixed on Him, focusing above, not ahead or behind. Stay in the zone of protection from God, understanding that the God we serve is a God of completion and it has already been done. So, we must line up with His predestined purpose in Christ for our lives here on earth, as it is

The N.O.W. Experience: 720* DEGREE TURN

in heaven. God is patiently waiting, but we must act NOW to obtain what He has for us NOW as we allow Him to order our steps willingly. We must plow a straight line with our eye on the cornerstone of faith. He who began a work in us (Philippians 1:6) is with us and knows the path He has for us to follow. He will show us the way even when tempted (1 Corinthians 10:13) for our steps are ordered by the Lord (Psalms 37:23) so we live in Him and walk with Him (Galatians 5:16) as it is reserved in heaven (1 Peter 1:4) sent from heaven (vs. 12). This is simple, Jesus is the light and the light changes things, so we must walk in the light because we are called to the light

(1 Pet 2: 9-10). The word is the light that shines in our minds (2 Peter 1:19) to keep us focused and ready for whatever comes our way, and we are called out of darkness into light

(1 Peter 2:9).

As we begin to live under the protection of Him, we will become victorious by renewing our minds, changing the way we walk and talk, and remembering that the unifying principle in all of this is our thinking. The way we think sets the standard for the battle. If we think we have lost, then we will lose and if we think we can't, then we won't. If we think we are crazy, then that is exactly what we will eventually be and on and on the vicious cycle goes. It is especially important that we have the attitude of Christ so we can win the battle set before us in finding our God given purpose. So, in our new form we must exemplify the new man, with new

The N.O.W. Experience: 720* DEGREE TURN

minds, new ways and doing things exactly as Christ would. By God's unmerited favor, we have a new lease on life and no longer are captive to fear, pain and doubt, but can multiply our lives one hundred-fold and be victorious leaders in our purpose provoked by the Lord.

Chapter 4

Faith!

Family hope is defined as waiting for something with an expected end. Hope is making a conscious decision to believe that taking action to produce faith leads to having patience to wait on the outcome of our hope. Looking beyond our natural eyes or senses and being able to really trust God, His word, and His example to be true. Again, we refer to Hebrews 11:1 where it says, "Now faith is the substance of things hoped for, the evidence of things not seen." We must believe in something and it takes faith to believe what we cannot see. If we cannot see ourselves winning before we win, then we will fail and lose. Our purpose must be intact to go forward in achieving our dreams vision and God provoked

purpose to be successful. We have learned that God has put His mind in us and that we must acknowledge Him through faith and hope, the word in Psalms 37:23 says that "the steps of a *good* man are ordered by the Lord, and He delights in his way." Understand that God has ordered the path for our purpose and we can change the way of our thinking to be like Christ and begin to activate the principles of God in our lives. The word tells us in Proverbs 13:12, that, "hope deferred maketh the heart sick, but when desire comes, it is as a tree." Hope is meant to be fulfilled just like our purpose is because of the blood of Jesus on the cross. But it is still up to us to activate these principles and reach the

The N.O.W. Experience: 720* DEGREE TURN

substances of hope so that we can manifest that God's kingdom will come, and that His will be done on earth as it is in heaven.

This begins with His predestined purpose and hope founded by God's word and His principles put into action. Below are some easy steps we can practice manifesting our hope into substance.

1. Faith that produces belief requires us to decide to work it through

remembering God's goodness with praise and worship.

2. Belief that produces faith requires an action to be taken to develop that God type of faith.

3. Faith that produces substance requires patience to wait on God's timing for our purpose or substance to come.

God's desire must become our desires so that we can produce

The N.O.W. Experience: 720* DEGREE TURN

hope through remembering, praise, and being willing to work the principles over and over until God's time for us has come.

Here is an exercise that we can practice with immediate success. It's called R.E.P.O.H.

This principle can take a bad habit and change it into a good habit or vice versa. It all depends on the user, but it goes like this:

The N.O.W. Experience: 720* DEGREE TURN

Repetition - anything done repeatedly will become

Easy - once anything becomes easy to do, it will be done with

Pleasure - once anything becomes pleasurable to do, it will be done

Often - once anything is done over and over, it will become a

Habit - good or bad

Becoming Christ like and Christ minded takes a lot of work, but it can be done.

The N.O.W. Experience: 720* DEGREE TURN

When you think like Him, your feelings are formed by Him, your actions are like His and you make choices like He would. Where He has already ordered our steps, we know that God has already planned our purpose in life from end to beginning. Our purpose is just to get in line with His anointed purpose that has already been completed in heaven, that it can be transferred here on earth for our lives. As we abide in Him and His grace, we can do the work and live holy. So, as we begin to make right choices, then Jesus can lead us to doing God's will as part of our purpose. God chose us in Him before the world was formed, so as we choose Him NOW (0 – 5 seconds.) we can live victorious on earth as it is in heaven!

The N.O.W. Experience: 720* DEGREE TURN

Chapter 5

Beliefs – Thoughts – Feelings

Ok in step five we find ourselves completing the task of finding our purpose in Godly living. Still, we must understand that this war continues until we are received into God's glory. As we continue to be formed and motivated by God, we must continue to win the fight of faith. Our decisions must lead to us reaching our potential and perfect will for our Christian lives. The word tells us in Proverbs 16:3 to commit your ways to the Lord and your thoughts will be established. See, we can become Godly thinkers that will develop our beliefs, thoughts, and feelings to be led by God's word, God's spirit and His ways. By believing and trusting in God to be the source of our hopes, our thinking will be sustained by the word and our purpose will begin to be seen from the inside that we can live it on the outside through our B-T-F'S (Beliefs, thoughts, and feelings).

The N.O.W. Experience: 720* DEGREE TURN

Let us explore the three types of believers to help find our purpose and identify what changes need to be made.

1. Thinkers – those that trust God completely and allow our thinking to guide our beliefs, feelings, and actions to be of God.

2. Feelers – those of us led by our emotions and senses that lead us to distorted actions. Remember that our senses cannot be trusted.

3. Actors- those who go through life making choices without thinking them out or the consequences.

Look at how we act when we follow God and how we act when not operating under the spirit. We can choose to stay conscious or look like those who fail that are led by the world's way. The word clearly warns us in Matthew 23:25-28 "Woe to you, scribes and Pharisees, hypocrites! For you cleanse the outside of the cup and dish, but inside they are full of extortion and self-indulgence. Blind Pharisee first cleanse the inside of the cup and dish, that the outside of them may be clean also. Woe to you, scribes and Pharisees, hypocrites! For you are like whitewashed tombs which indeed appear beautiful outwardly, but inside are full of dead *men*'s bones and all uncleanness. Even so you also outwardly appear righteous to men, but inside you are full of hypocrisy and lawlessness." This is a prime example from Christ that it doesn't matter what's on the outside. We can wear all the fines clothes, large crosses and lapel pins with Jesus written all over them, but if we are not cleansed and purposed driven by God that we are considered hypocrites just like the scribes and Pharisees mentioned in Matthew 23. The word of God also tells us in 1 John 3:24 that, he who keeps His commandments abides in Him, and He in him. And by this, we know that He abides in us, by the Spirit whom He has given us. It all comes from God and if we allow Him in our hearts and minds, we will be strengthened in our way of thinking, feeling, and acting. The word also tells us in John 15:1-5 that, "I am the true vine, and My Father is the vinedresser. ²"Every branch in Me that does not bear fruit He takes away; and every *branch* that bears fruit He prunes, that it may bear more fruit. ³"You are already clean because of the word which I have spoken to you. ⁴"Abide in Me, and I in you. As the branch cannot bear fruit of itself, unless it abides in the vine, neither can you, unless you abide in Me. ⁵"I am the vine, you *are* the branches. He who abides in Me, and I in

The N.O.W. Experience: 720* DEGREE TURN

him, bears much fruit; for without Me you can do nothing." Now, can we perceive this instruction directly from God to us, to live in Him and allow His direction to guide our every move? We must stay focused on the Lord and let our thoughts be fixed on Him every moment of the day. Meditating on His word and staying in constant prayer without ceasing. To hear Him is to know Him, then and only then can we be led by God in our purpose and calling. We must stay focused so we can do what God has for us to do, so His blessings

The N.O.W. Experience: 720* DEGREE TURN

will overtake us. All we can desire can come to pass and be ours if we will find our Godly purpose and be provoked into action to walk with God.

The N.O.W. Experience: 720* DEGREE TURN

Chapter 6

The Turn

Family the turn is the complete release of self-control, no longer thinking, acting, or moving without the will of God. John 3:30 clearly states that "HE must increase, and I must decrease". God cannot be increased until we decrease. He will not move until we do. Every second we must be dedicated to death of self in order to truly experience the move of God. The 720-degree turn

The N.O.W. Experience: 720* DEGREE TURN

is a way of completing the task and walking under the authority of God. Turning 720 degrees means turning 360 degrees from self and doing a 360 degree turn to God.

The true meaning of the principle is found in John chapter 15. We learn not only how to turn, additionally we learn the way to stay in the turning lane. First, Jesus identifies himself as the true vine whose connection comes from the vinedresser, which is God who is in heaven.

Second, we are put on immediate notice that if we are not productive, we are removed, but if we produce, He prunes us for the greater ability to produce more.

Third, we are told to not worry about anything, but the word spoken to us that cleanses us because He said it. Period.

Fourth, if we abide in Him only, we must stay connected, as He is the only thing worthy to come in to assist in productivity. John 15:4 "Abide in Me, and I in you. As the branch cannot bear fruit of itself, unless it abides in the vine, neither can you, unless you abide in Me." It's simple when we agree with the word, walk in the word and live the word.

We must recognize the worth in going after Christ:

- It's not about me
- It's all about God
- With Him – I can do all things
- Without Him – I fail

And begin to model our walk so that it resembles Christ and follow His divine example of bearing much fruit, (John 15:5) with Him as the lead. If we decide to do it on our own, we will never see the light that shines on the darkness in our lives and the fires burns us away instead of setting on us as a consuming fire (Hebrews 12:29). "For our God is a consuming fire."

Fifth, if His words abide in us, then our communication is clear, understood, and answered immediately according to

The N.O.W. Experience: 720* DEGREE TURN

God's will. See the turn exemplifies the will of God, for His glory so that we become true followers of Jesus. NOW is the time to go higher, deeper, wider, longer than you ever have before in our turning completely to God. Connection with God has nothing to do with pain, hate or suffering. It's full of love. Jesus explains clearly in John 15:9 that as the Father loved Him so He loves us that we may abide in His love continuously. If we keep His commandments of love will abide in this love and joy shall makes us full. Now understand that turning

The N.O.W. Experience: 720* DEGREE TURN

completely to GOD and completely from self now elevates you to a different position. We are no longer considered servants, but friends. Friends of Jesus to now do the work of loving each other unconditionally (John 14:11-15) as we have been commanded. Look at Mark 12:31 that teaches us "You shall love your neighbor as yourself. There is no other commandment greater than these." And in (1 Peter 4:8) Love not only covers a multitude of sin. but LOVE chose us, not the other way around of us choosing HIM. Jesus chose

The N.O.W. Experience: 720* DEGREE TURN

us. Jesus appointed us. And yes, YOU are too. That we should go and bear much to share with others, not to just give in a time of need, but strengthen one another to also become productive. We line up, we get it almost together, and then all hell breaks loose. Yes, that is the process. Turning completely to God upsets this world. Us being on one accord is not respected by this world. But turning completely to God is an encouragement of our faith, walking not by sight, but by the spirit. Finding our place in God and experiencing His

The N.O.W. Experience: 720* DEGREE TURN

fullness and sharing His love. See, we must reach Him where He is. Then and only then does the helper fall from heaven, testifies of God and bears witness with us because of our willingness to turn and exercise our authority as children of God. So, we are here, and the journey begins. Finally, "I'm strong in the LORD and the power of His might..." (Ephesians 6:10). "I can do all things through Jesus Christ whom strengthens me" (Philippians 4:13). Now, we cannot lose focus and miss the mark. No, it is important to stay on

The N.O.W. Experience: 720* DEGREE TURN

point. Beginning now and all seasons to come, we must stay the course, do the will of God, and press towards the mark of the high calling!

The N.O.W. Experience: 720* DEGREE TURN

Pastor E. has dedicated over 37 years to the ministry promoting Jesus Christ after receiving his call into the ministry in his early 20's. In 2000, Pastor E. founded the Provoked to Purpose Ministries ~ P2P Ministries. Teaching and equipping the saints for the work of the ministry while guiding the saved to be provoked to do God's will and reaching the unsaved to be provoked to doing God's will is the mission of P2P. Under Pastor E's leadership, the ministry continues to grow as he works with diverse community-focused organizations and builds strategic alliances with likeminded ministries.

Dr. Edward Hamilton

The N.O.W. Experience: 720* DEGREE TURN

In 2014, Pastor E. launched the N.O.W (Not Our Will) Network with a quest to reach more people by offering a Christian Programming Network as an avenue for like-minded believers with God inspired messages. The blog talk radio broadcast network is host to several shows focusing on the growth of God's people.

To learn more about Pastor E, P2P Community Development, or our covering ETEEZ4UNOW or the N.O.W Network, please visit www.provoked2000now.com
(562) 413-3710

Made in the USA
Middletown, DE
24 September 2022

10934993R00064